Cyber Security Risk Management

About the Author

With over two decades of dedicated experience in the realm of digital security, the author stands as a leading voice in cybersecurity risk management. Armed with a distinguished military background in Communications and IT, they bring a unique perspective that combines military discipline with profound industry expertise. This robust foundation has equipped them to navigate the complexities of cybersecurity, making them not only a trusted expert but also a passionate advocate for organizational security in an increasingly digital world.

The author's professional journey spans a commendable 20 to 23 years, encompassing collaborations with both local and central government departments across the UK. Their extensive background includes developing and implementing advanced security controls to protect organizations from shifting threats. Their ability to operate independently, as well as within high-profile institutions, has honed their capabilities and insights, positioning them as a key contributor in cybersecurity discussions and initiatives aimed at safeguarding sensitive information.

Educationally, the author is well grounded with qualifications that complement their practical experience, providing a theoretical framework to their hands-on skills. Their journey into writing has been fueled by the realization that effective communication of complex cybersecurity concepts is essential. This book is a manifestation of their commitment to demystifying cybersecurity for a broader audience, merging academic rigor with real-world application to engage and inform readers.

In addition to their technical acumen, the author's writing style is characterized by clarity and accessibility. They strive to make intricate subjects understandable, ensuring that individuals from diverse backgrounds can grasp crucial cybersecurity principles. Their genuine passion for teaching and sharing knowledge infuses their work, resonating with readers who might feel overwhelmed by the intricacies of digital security.

As a future-focused author, they are driven by a mission to elevate awareness of cybersecurity's critical importance. Their aim is to inspire resilience and proactive strategies within organizations and individuals alike. Through writing, consulting, and speaking engagements, they aspire to create a safer digital landscape, continually seeking opportunities to share expertise and engage with emerging cybersecurity challenges.

Table of Contents

Chapter 1: Introduction to Cyber Security Risk Management

Chapter 2: The Cyber Threat Landscape

Chapter 3: Risk Management Frameworks

Chapter 4: Risk Identification Techniques

(1) - 4.1: Asset Identification

(2) - 4.2: Vulnerability Assessment

(3) - 4.3: Threat Modelling Approaches

Chapter 5: Risk Assessment Processes

Chapter 6: Risk Prioritization Strategies

Chapter 7: Risk Mitigation Techniques

Chapter 8: Risk Acceptance and Transfer

Chapter 9: Monitoring and Reviewing Risks

(1) - 9.1: Continuous Risk Monitoring Techniques

(2) - 9.2: Metrics and Key Performance Indicators

(3) - 9.3: Conducting Regular Risk Reviews

Chapter 10: Compliance and Legal Considerations

Chapter 11: Risk Communication and Reporting

Chapter 12: Cyber Security Governance

(1) - 12.1: Establishing a Governance Framework

(2) - 12.2: Roles and Responsibilities in Risk Management

(3) - 12.3: Governance Processes and Policies

Chapter 13: Incident Management and Response

Chapter 14: Future Trends in Cyber Security Risk Management

(1) - 14.1: Machine Learning and AI in Risk Management

(2) - 14.2: The Impact of Quantum Computing

(3) - 14.3: Evolving Cyber Security Landscape

Chapter 15: Case Studies in Risk Management

(1) - 15.1: Successful Risk Management Implementations

(2) - 15.2: Lessons Learned from Cyber Incidents

(3) - 15.3: Industry-specific Risk Management Analyses

Chapter 1: Introduction to Cyber Security Risk Management

1.1: Definition and Importance

Cyber Security Risk Management refers to the process of identifying, assessing, and prioritizing potential risks to an organization's information assets, followed by the coordinated application of resources to minimize, monitor, and control the probability or impact of unfortunate events. This function plays a critical role in protecting an organization's assets, especially as the digital landscape continues to evolve. Digital assets, including sensitive data and proprietary information, are invaluable, and their protection through effective risk management strategies becomes paramount. The discipline bridges the gap between technology and operational practices, ensuring that all aspects of the organization are aligned for a holistic approach to risk mitigation. Cyber Security Risk Management not only safeguards against potential breaches but also fortifies the trust of clients and stakeholders in the organization's ability to protect their data.

The importance of proactive risk management cannot be overstated. By adopting a forward-thinking approach, organizations can stay ahead of cyber threats which are constantly evolving in complexity and sophistication. A proactive stance allows for the identification of vulnerabilities before they can be exploited, significantly reducing the likelihood of breaches and the subsequent financial and reputational damage that can ensue. Implementing regular risk assessments and incident response planning positions organizations to react swiftly and effectively in the event of a cyber incident. Moreover, proactive risk management fosters a culture of security awareness within the organization, empowering employees to recognize and report potential threats, thereby enhancing the overall security posture. Cyber threats are persistent; therefore, an organization's ability to anticipate and manage these risks is crucial for its long-term success.

Understanding the dynamic nature of cyber threats and the importance of a comprehensive risk management framework is essential for fostering resilience. Employing tools and technologies to assess risks regularly, coupled with thorough training for all employees, ensures that the organization is well-equipped to handle potential challenges. Always remember that risk management in cybersecurity is not a one-time effort but an ongoing process that demands commitment and continual improvement.

1.2: Historical Context and Evolution

The historical development of cyber security risk management practices has evolved significantly over the decades, shaped by technological advancements and the increasing sophistication of cyber threats. In the early days of computing, security was often an afterthought. Systems were small, isolated, and not connected; thus, risk management was minimalistic and generally focused on physical security. As networks became more prevalent in the 1990s, the emergence of the internet introduced new vulnerabilities. This era saw the creation of various security frameworks, including early versions of ISO standards, which began to formalize risk assessment processes.

The turn of the millennium brought the rise of cyber incidents that captured public attention and ignited a sense of urgency within organizations to adopt more robust risk management practices. Notable events like the Melissa virus, the I LOVE YOU worm, and the 2000 DoS attacks on major websites highlighted the dire consequences of inadequate cybersecurity. In response to these incidents, frameworks began to evolve—approaches like the NIST Cybersecurity Framework sought to provide organizations with structured methodologies for identifying, assessing, and mitigating cyber risks. Over the years, lessons learned from incidents have fine-tuned these frameworks, leading to more comprehensive risk management strategies that encompass both technical defenses and human factors.

Moreover, past cyber incidents have had a profound impact on shaping current risk management approaches. For instance, high-profile breaches such as the Target breach in 2013 and the Equifax incident in 2017 underscored the need for organizations to look beyond traditional IT security and consider broader implications, including supply chain risks and data privacy regulations like GDPR. These events forced organizations to adopt a proactive approach, emphasizing continuous monitoring, incident response planning, and regular assessments of both physical and virtual environments. As cyber threats continue to evolve, risk management practices must remain agile, integrating lessons from history to anticipate future challenges. Maintaining a culture of awareness and preparedness within organizations can significantly bolster defenses against emerging threats.

1.3: Key Concepts and Terminology

In the context of cyber security, understanding key terms is essential for effective risk management. Risk refers to the potential for loss or damage when a threat exploits a vulnerability. Vulnerability is a weakness that can be targeted by an attacker, while a threat is any circumstance that has the potential to cause harm, such as cyberattacks or natural disasters. Impact describes the consequences that occur if a risk materializes, often measured in terms of financial loss, reputational damage, or operational disruption. Grasping these definitions allows security professionals to better assess their organization's risk landscape.

Important concepts like the risk management cycle provide a structured approach to identifying, analyzing, and mitigating risks. This cycle typically consists of several phases, including risk assessment, risk treatment, and risk monitoring. Each phase has specific objectives and outcomes that contribute to a comprehensive risk management strategy. Stakeholder roles are crucial throughout this process. Security professionals must collaborate with various stakeholders, including senior management, IT personnel, and external partners, to ensure that risks are effectively addressed. Engaging stakeholders not only fosters a culture of security but also enhances the overall resilience of the organization against cyber threats.

As you navigate the complex landscape of cyber security risk management, remember that continuous learning and adaptation are key. Keeping up-to-date with emerging threats and evolving industry best practices will empower you to make informed decisions that protect your organization's assets.

Chapter 2: The Cyber Threat Landscape

2.1: Overview of Cyber Threats

Organizations today face an array of cyber threats that continuously evolve as technology advances. One of the most prevalent types of threat is malware, which encompasses viruses, worms, trojans, and ransomware. These malicious programs can infiltrate systems, damage data integrity, and disrupt operations, often demanding a ransom for restoring access to encrypted information. Phishing attempts are another major concern, where attackers use deceptive emails or websites to trick users into revealing sensitive information such as login credentials or financial details. Furthermore, distributed denial-of-service (DDoS) attacks overwhelm networks with excessive traffic, rendering services inoperable and causing significant downtime for businesses. Additionally, insider threats present a unique challenge, as employees or contractors with access to sensitive systems can intentionally or unintentionally cause harm or leak data. As organizations increasingly adopt cloud services, vulnerabilities associated with these platforms and third-party integrations also pose considerable risk, necessitating robust security measures across all digital domains.

The motivations behind cyber attacks can vary significantly, ranging from financial gain to political statements or personal vendettas. Cybercriminals often aim to exploit vulnerabilities for monetary gain through theft, extortion, or fraud. Passionate hacktivists may target organizations to make a political statement, while state-sponsored attacks focus on espionage, seeking to acquire sensitive information to gain strategic advantages. The implications of these attacks on business operations are profound. A successful cyber breach can lead to significant financial losses, reputational damage, and legal ramifications as companies face increasing scrutiny from stakeholders and regulatory bodies. The repercussions extend beyond immediate losses; long-term trust and customer loyalty can be severely compromised. Organizations must not only address the technical aspects of risk management but also consider the broader impact of cyber threats on their overall business strategy and practices.

To effectively combat these threats, it is essential for organizations to cultivate a robust cybersecurity culture. Employees should be educated on the potential risks and best practices, fostering an environment where security is a shared responsibility. Implementing layered security measures, such as firewalls, intrusion detection systems, and regular software updates can greatly bolster defenses against cyber attacks. Organizations should also conduct regular risk assessments, which help to identify vulnerabilities and develop strategies tailored to mitigate specific risks. By understanding the landscape of cyber threats and their motivations, cybersecurity professionals can better equip their organizations to withstand and respond to incidents, ultimately safeguarding their critical assets and ensuring long-term operational resilience.

2.2: Understanding Cyber Attack Vectors

Cybercriminals constantly evolve their tactics, often relying on a variety of attack vectors that exploit existing vulnerabilities within an organization's security landscape. One of the most common vectors is phishing, where attackers trick individuals into revealing sensitive information through seemingly legitimate emails or websites. Likewise, malware delivery through malicious attachments or links further demonstrates how cybercriminals gain unauthorized access to systems. Often, an attacker leverages server vulnerabilities by using techniques such as SQL injection or cross-site scripting, effectively embedding harmful code within applications to compromise data integrity and confidentiality. Additionally, insider threats pose a significant risk, as trusted employees may inadvertently or intentionally breach security protocols, leading to devastating outcomes. As organizations transition to cloud environments, the complexities of infrastructure can expand attack surfaces, creating gaps in security where unauthorized users can exploit cloud configurations or lack of authentication measures.

Consider the infamous Target breach in 2013, where attackers accessed payment card information through a third-party vendor. Attackers used stolen credentials to enter Target's network, highlighting how even trusted partnerships can become vectors for cyber threats. Another dramatic illustration is the 2017 Equifax data breach, resulting from an unpatched vulnerability in the Apache Struts web application framework. This incident not only exposed sensitive consumer data but also demonstrated how a failure to regularly update and patch systems can serve as an open door for attackers. Real-world cases like these emphasize the importance of understanding and mitigating the various ways cybercriminals can exploit network vulnerabilities. Prevention strategies often center around continuous monitoring and incident response plans in tandem with comprehensive security training for employees.

It's crucial for cyber security professionals to stay vigilant and informed about the evolving tactics used by cybercriminals. Implementing layered security measures, conducting regular vulnerability assessments, and fostering a proactive security culture within the organization can significantly reduce the likelihood of successful attacks. Encourage teams to engage in tabletop exercises that simulate attack scenarios to better prepare for potential breaches. This preparation not only enhances awareness but also solidifies a coordinated response strategy, ultimately strengthening the entire cyber defense posture.

2.3: Emerging Threats and Trends

Ransomware attacks have surged in recent years, becoming a significant concern for organizations across all sectors. These attacks often involve hackers encrypting vital data and demanding a ransom for its release. Phishing schemes continue to evolve, becoming increasingly sophisticated and deceptive, leading individuals into believing they are interacting with trusted entities. This manipulation often results in unauthorized access to sensitive information. Insider threats are gaining attention as well, where employees, whether maliciously or inadvertently, leak sensitive data or compromise systems. The motivations behind insider threats can range from financial gain to simple negligence, making them particularly complex to identify and mitigate.

The rapid evolution of technology brings both advantages and challenges, creating new hurdles for risk management in cybersecurity. For instance, the rise of cloud computing and Internet of Things (IoT) devices has expanded attack surfaces, leaving organizations vulnerable to breaches from unprotected endpoints. Artificial intelligence and machine learning can be double-edged swords; while they enhance detection capabilities, they also enable attackers to bypass traditional security measures by automating attacks. Furthermore, the integration of advanced technologies often means that cybersecurity professionals must continuously adapt their strategies and policies. Staying ahead of emerging threats is essential, as is developing a proactive culture that prioritizes cybersecurity awareness and resilience.

Investing in employee training and awareness programs can significantly reduce the risks associated with these emerging threats. Regular simulations of phishing attacks can help employees recognize and report suspicious activities. Additionally, adopting a layered security approach, which includes endpoint protection, network security, and regular vulnerability assessments, can create a robust defense against various cyber threats. As technology continues to advance, maintaining a vigilant and agile risk management strategy will be imperative for organizations aiming to safeguard their critical assets.

Chapter 3: Risk Management Frameworks

3.1: NIST Risk Management Framework

The NIST Risk Management Framework (RMF) is a structured process that integrates security, privacy, and risk management activities into the system development life cycle. By establishing a clear set of guidelines, the RMF enables organizations to effectively manage information security risks. This framework consists of several key components, including categorization of information systems, selection of security controls, implementation of those controls, assessment of security controls, authorization of information system operation, and ongoing monitoring of security controls. Each of these components plays a vital role in creating a comprehensive risk management strategy that aligns with organizational goals and compliance requirements. In organizational settings, applying this framework helps teams systematically identify and mitigate risks that could potentially harm information assets, ensuring that security measures are not just reactive but proactive in nature.

Utilizing the NIST framework offers a variety of benefits, particularly for organizations striving for a structured approach to risk management. Primarily, it provides a repeatable and scalable process that can be tailored to fit any organization, regardless of size or industry. This flexibility allows teams to address specific threats and vulnerabilities while remaining consistent with federal standards and best practices. Additionally, implementing the RMF fosters a culture of security within an organization, encouraging collaboration among various departments. By breaking down silos and promoting shared responsibility for security, the NIST framework enhances overall resilience against cybersecurity threats. Furthermore, adopting this framework can lead to improved compliance with regulations and a clearer understanding of risk management priorities. Organizations that leverage the RMF can better allocate resources to critical security initiatives, effectively reduce risks, and ultimately safeguard their information assets.

Integrating the NIST Risk Management Framework into an organization not only enhances security posture but also positions the organization to respond effectively to emerging threats. Keeping abreast of updates and evolving best practices within the NIST guidance can provide ongoing improvements in risk management strategies. Cybersecurity professionals should continuously analyze the effectiveness of the applied controls and adapt as necessary, ensuring metrics are established for consistent evaluation. Building a strong foundation with the RMF today can prepare organizations for the challenges of tomorrow.

3.2: ISO/IEC 27001 Standards

ISO/IEC 27001 is a globally recognized standard that specifies the requirements for establishing, implementing, maintaining, and continually improving an information security management system (ISMS). This standard is essential for organizations seeking to effectively manage their information security risks and protect sensitive data. By adopting ISO/IEC 27001, businesses demonstrate their commitment to safeguarding information assets, which is increasingly vital in a world where cyber threats are pervasive. The relevance of these standards extends beyond compliance; they promote a culture of security within organizations, encouraging proactive measures in risk management and enhancing overall resilience against potential security breaches.

The process for achieving ISO/IEC 27001 certification involves several key steps that organizations must navigate to establish a robust ISMS. Initial steps include conducting a comprehensive risk assessment, developing a security policy, and defining the scope of the ISMS. Organizations then implement controls aimed at mitigating identified risks, followed by internal audits and management reviews to ensure continuous improvement. Achieving certification not only enhances the organization's credibility but also brings numerous advantages, such as increased customer trust, compliance with legal and regulatory requirements, and improved operational efficiency. Moreover, ISO/IEC 27001 certification can set organizations apart from competitors by showcasing their dedication to information security excellence, ultimately leading to greater business opportunities.

An important practical tip for organizations aiming for ISO/IEC 27001 compliance is to foster a culture of security awareness among all employees. Effective training and communication about the importance of information security can significantly contribute to the success of the ISMS. It is essential for every employee to understand their role in protecting the organization's information, as human factors often represent the weakest link in security. Therefore, organizations should prioritize ongoing education and awareness initiatives as part of their journey towards a successful ISO/IEC 27001 certification.

3.3: FAIR Model Analysis

The Factor Analysis of Information Risk (FAIR) model provides a structured framework for understanding and quantifying information risk. It breaks down risk into its key components, allowing professionals to analyze and express the impact and likelihood of various threat scenarios in specific financial terms. By focusing on measurable factors such as loss event frequency and probable loss magnitude, the FAIR model helps organizations move away from vague assessments of risk and towards a more precise understanding of potential financial impacts. This clear quantification is crucial in environments where resources are limited and decisions must be backed by data. Utilizing FAIR allows cybersecurity professionals to evaluate risk in a way that assists in prioritizing actions based on the potential financial implications, compared to merely the qualitative assessments that have traditionally dominated risk conversations.

The implementation of the FAIR model enhances decision-making around security investments in a meaningful way. By quantifying risk, security teams can provide concrete numbers that define the return on investment for various security controls or initiatives. For instance, rather than simply arguing for a larger budget based on fear of breaches, a team can present a calculated analysis showing how investing in a specific technology might mitigate risks of a dollar figure that could result from a breach. This analytical approach supports strategic planning and allows organizations to allocate funds in a manner that aligns with business objectives. When resources are dedicated according to the level of risk and potential return, it creates an environment where security investments can directly correlate to improved organizational resilience.

Understanding and applying the FAIR model not only aids in justifying existing security budgets but also in developing future cyber strategies. By consistently evaluating and adjusting risk assessments using this model, organizations can stay agile and informed on risk changes. A practical tip is to regularly review the risk assessments as the threat landscape evolves, ensuring that the risk quantifications remain relevant and actionable. This proactive approach will keep your organization ahead of the curve, making security investments that are both financially sound and strategically aligned.

Chapter 4: Risk Identification Techniques

4.1: Asset Identification

Identifying critical assets within an organization is paramount in shaping a robust cyber security posture. These assets, which may range from sensitive data repositories and intellectual property to essential infrastructure, form the backbone of business operations. The significance of asset identification lies in its ability to help organizations understand what they need to protect. Without a clear identification of these assets, efforts to mitigate risks can become misguided, leading to inefficient resource allocation and potential exposure to threats. In a world where cyber threats are ever-evolving, knowing the critical assets that require protection helps in establishing priorities, fostering strategic planning, and enhancing overall risk management strategies.

Effective methods for cataloguing these assets create a structured approach that aids in risk management. One common technique is the implementation of an asset inventory management system. This method involves not only listing assets but also categorizing them based on their criticality and the potential impact of their loss or compromise. Organizations can utilize automated discovery tools to facilitate this process, allowing for real-time visibility into their digital environment. Regular audits and updates of this inventory are crucial, ensuring that any new assets are documented and properly assessed for risk. By understanding the context in which these assets operate—such as their interdependencies and the environments in which they function—organizations can more accurately gauge their vulnerability and the necessary protective measures that should be employed.

Cultivating a culture of continuous improvement regarding asset management is essential. Teams should invest time in training staff on the importance of asset identification and encourage an ongoing dialogue about changes that may affect assets. Collaborating across departments can lead to more comprehensive asset identification, ensuring that both IT and operational perspectives are considered. Cyber security professionals can leverage frameworks like the NIST Cybersecurity Framework, which emphasizes asset management as a key component in risk management. Remember, treating asset identification as an ongoing process rather than a one-time task aids in maintaining security resilience, proactively identifying gaps and adapting to threats.

4.2: Vulnerability Assessment

Conducting a vulnerability assessment is a vital process for identifying weaknesses in systems, allowing organizations to fortify their defenses against potential attacks. The assessment begins with the gathering of pertinent information about the systems in question, followed by a thorough analysis to pinpoint vulnerabilities. This process often includes techniques such as asset discovery, where all devices, applications, and services are catalogued. Understanding the environment is crucial; it helps establish a baseline for detecting anomalies. Once the assets are identified, next comes the vulnerability analysis phase, where tools scan for known weaknesses and configuration errors. This phase is usually accompanied by an evaluation of the potential impact these vulnerabilities may pose, helping prioritize remediation efforts based on risk assessment. Overall, a structured approach ensures that vulnerabilities are assessed continuously and systematically, encouraging proactive management instead of reactive responses.

Utilizing effective tools and methodologies during vulnerability scanning can significantly enhance the discovery and management of security weaknesses. Common tools vary from open-source options like OpenVAS and Nessus to enterprise solutions like Qualys and Rapid7. Each tool has its unique features, such as web application scanning, network scanning, and even patch management integrations. Methodologies often incorporate industry standards like OWASP Top Ten and NIST frameworks to ensure thorough coverage. For more nuanced assessments, professionals may use a combination of static and dynamic analysis techniques. Static analysis evaluates source code without executing it, while dynamic analysis inspects applications while they are running. Additionally, employing threat intelligence feeds can help in correlating vulnerabilities with real-world exploits, providing context to the severity of risks faced. This layered approach ensures a comprehensive assessment, reducing the likelihood of undetected weaknesses.

To stay ahead of potential threats, it is essential to adopt a continuous vulnerability management strategy. Regular scanning, combined with periodic manual assessments, helps keep pace with evolving threats and newly discovered vulnerabilities. Engage with your security team to develop policies that mandate regular assessments and ensure that identified vulnerabilities are tracked and remediated promptly. Creating a culture of awareness about vulnerabilities and making security everyone's responsibility is invaluable. By adopting these practices, you not only improve your organization's security posture but also build resilience against ever-changing threats.

4.3: Threat Modelling Approaches

The landscape of cyber threats is continually evolving, making it essential for organizations to utilize various threat modelling techniques to anticipate potential attacks. One prominent approach is the STRIDE model, which focuses on identifying six types of threats: Spoofing, Tampering, Repudiation, Information Disclosure, Denial of Service, and Elevation of Privilege. By systematically analyzing a system through these categories, security professionals can gain a comprehensive understanding of vulnerabilities and possible exploitation methods. Another effective technique is Attack Trees, which visually represent the paths an attacker might take to achieve their goals. This method not only highlights potential weaknesses but also helps prioritize security requirements based on the severity and likelihood of different attack vectors. Additionally, the PASTA framework, or Process for Attack Simulation and Threat Analysis, emphasizes a risk-centric methodology that begins by aligning security threats with business objectives, facilitating a more effective threat response tailored to organizational needs.

Examining successful case studies can shed light on the practical applications of these techniques. For instance, a financial institution faced a significant threat of data breaches. By implementing the STRIDE model, they mapped out potential attack scenarios and identified critical vulnerabilities within their systems. This proactive measure led to substantial investment in secure coding practices and access control measures, substantially reducing their attack surface. Another example involves a technology firm that utilized Attack Trees to analyze a planned product launch. They discovered potential exploitation points that could be targeted by malicious actors and were able to address these weaknesses prior to the product's release, thus gaining a competitive advantage by ensuring a secure launch. These examples highlight how effective threat modelling can not only safeguard assets but also enhance an organization's reputation and customer trust.

Incorporating threat modelling into the risk management discipline can significantly bolster an organization's cybersecurity posture. Professionals should engage in regular threat assessments, leveraging a combination of modelling techniques to ensure a well-rounded approach to security. Establishing a culture of continuous improvement around security practices is crucial, as it allows organizations to remain agile and adaptive in the face of emerging threats. Investing in training staff to recognize and act upon potential security threats can serve as a vital component of an overall security strategy, where every employee plays a role in preserving the integrity of sensitive information and systems.

Chapter 5: Risk Assessment Processes

5.1: Qualitative vs. Quantitative Assessment

Qualitative and quantitative assessment methods serve as two fundamental approaches in risk management, each with its unique strengths and weaknesses. Qualitative assessments focus on descriptive and subjective data, often gathering insights through interviews, focus groups, or expert opinions. This approach is particularly effective in situations where numerical data may be scarce or difficult to gather. It offers a nuanced understanding of risks by capturing the human aspect of threats, vulnerabilities, and controls. In contexts such as assessing insider threats or the impact of a new security policy, qualitative assessments provide rich, contextual insights that quantitative methods may overlook. Conversely, quantitative assessments involve numeric data and statistics, providing a more objective analysis of risk scenarios. These methods utilize metrics and models, making them suitable for situations where precise measurements exist, such as analyzing incident frequency, financial loss estimates, or vulnerability counts. For circumstances requiring quick, data-driven decisions—like evaluating compliance with regulatory requirements or assessing technical controls—quantitative assessments become indispensable.

In practice, both qualitative and quantitative assessments contribute significantly to risk management decisions but in different ways. Qualitative approaches allow security professionals to explore and understand complex threats and the perceptions of various stakeholders. For instance, after a cyber incident, a qualitative review can help dissect the organizational response and identify areas for improvement. This approach can also highlight the training needs of personnel or the effectiveness of communication strategies during a breach. On the other hand, quantitative assessments often support more tactical decisions, such as prioritizing investments in security technologies based on data about the likelihood of various attack vectors. By employing statistical models, organizations can allocate resources more effectively by identifying the most likely and impactful risks, ensuring that the security strategy aligns with the risk appetite of the business.

Understanding both methodologies enhances decision-making in risk management. A balanced approach that leverages insights from qualitative assessments while underpinned by quantitative data can lead to more robust risk strategies. Professionals should consider integrating both methods to create a holistic view of the risk landscape, combining the depth of qualitative insights with the clarity and precision of quantitative data. Emphasizing flexibility in choosing the methods best suited to the context can improve response capabilities and overall risk management effectiveness.

5.2: Risk Analysis Methods

Understanding the various methodologies for conducting risk analysis is crucial for any cyber security professional engaging in risk management. Scenario analysis involves evaluating different hypothetical situations and their potential impacts on an organization's information systems. This method allows professionals to envision various threats scenarios, assessing how systems might respond and what consequences might ensue. On the other hand, sensitivity analysis focuses on identifying how sensitive the outputs of a given risk model are to changes in input variables. This can significantly aid in determining which risks have the most substantial impact on the organization and can help prioritize risk management efforts based on where changes could make the most difference.

Choosing the right analysis method hinges on an organization's specific needs, objectives, and the context of the risks being assessed. Factors such as the size of the organization, the complexity of its systems, and the regulatory environment all play a role in selecting the appropriate methodology. For smaller organizations with simpler systems, a straightforward scenario analysis may suffice. Larger organizations, particularly those with intricate systems and diverse operations, might benefit from a more comprehensive approach that combines different methodologies to capture a more nuanced understanding of risks. Ultimately, the goal is to ensure that the selected method aligns well with the organization's risk appetite and strategic objectives.

One practical tip for cyber security professionals is to maintain flexibility in your analysis approach. The landscape of risks is constantly evolving, influenced by emerging technologies and shifting threat landscapes. Regularly revisiting and adjusting your chosen methodology as new information becomes available will enhance your organization's ability to respond proactively to risks. Engaging cross-disciplinary teams in the analysis process can also provide broader perspectives, leading to more thorough risk insights.

5.3: Evaluating Risk Impact and Likelihood

Assessing the impact of risks and their likelihood of occurrence is a critical aspect of risk management in cybersecurity. The criteria for this assessment should include factors such as the potential financial loss, operational disruption, damage to reputation, and legal implications. By understanding the consequences associated with a risk, cybersecurity professionals can better prioritize which threats require immediate attention. Additionally, the likelihood of a risk manifesting must be evaluated based on historical data, current threat landscapes, and the effectiveness of existing security measures. A combination of qualitative and quantitative assessment methods can enhance this evaluation, allowing professionals to assign ratings or scores to both impact and likelihood. This structured approach helps in developing a more consistent understanding of the risk environment.

Risk quantification techniques play a vital role in prioritizing risk responses. Methods such as Risk Matrix, Monte Carlo simulations, and Value at Risk (VaR) are popular amongst cybersecurity professionals. The Risk Matrix provides a visual representation of risks based on their impact and likelihood, enabling teams to identify which risks are most critical. Monte Carlo simulations allow for complex assessments by running multiple scenarios to predict potential outcomes under varying conditions, thus painting a clearer picture of risk exposure. Value at Risk quantifies the potential loss in value of an asset or portfolio over a defined period for a given confidence interval, giving a clear figure that can be critically analyzed. These techniques enhance decision-making processes by not only informing about the severity of risks but also providing a foundation for a proactive risk management strategy.

Incorporating a methodical approach to evaluating risk impact and likelihood will enable cybersecurity professionals to allocate resources effectively and develop robust response strategies. Leveraging these evaluation methods creates a framework that not only identifies risks but also makes it possible to address them efficiently. A practical tip for security teams is to regularly review and update their risk assessments, as the cybersecurity landscape evolves rapidly. Keeping up with new threats and adjusting impact and likelihood evaluations accordingly ensures a more resilient risk management strategy.

Chapter 6: Risk Prioritization Strategies

6.1: Risk Scoring Systems

Risk scoring systems play a crucial role in identifying and prioritizing risks within an organization. Various models exist that help cybersecurity professionals categorize vulnerabilities and threats based on their potential impact and likelihood. Common systems include qualitative and quantitative scoring methods, such as the Common Vulnerability Scoring System (CVSS), which provides a standardized frame for assessing security vulnerabilities. Additionally, frameworks like FAIR (Factor Analysis of Information Risk) offer a more comprehensive approach by evaluating risks in terms of financial impact. These scoring systems enable professionals to quantify risks, thereby facilitating informed decision-making on security measures. Choosing the right risk scoring model can significantly affect how effectively an organization can allocate resources to mitigate identified risks.

Customization of risk scorecards is vital to align the scoring system with organizational priorities and specific contexts. A one-size-fits-all approach may lead to misaligned risk assessments that do not accurately reflect an organization's unique vulnerabilities and business objectives. For example, organizations in highly regulated industries may place greater emphasis on compliance risks, while technology firms might focus more on innovation-related threats. By tailoring risk scoring systems, organizations can ensure that their scorecards prioritize what is truly important to their operations and strategic goals. This customization not only improves risk visibility but also enhances buy-in from stakeholders, making it crucial for effective risk management.

To optimize the effectiveness of risk scoring systems, cybersecurity professionals should regularly review and update their scoring criteria and weighting. Cyber threats evolve rapidly, and so should the methodologies used to assess them. Continuous engagement with business units can further refine what aspects of risk should be prioritized, creating a proactive rather than reactive risk management environment. Maintaining a dynamic risk scoring system allows an organization to stay ahead of emerging threats and ensure that its security strategy remains aligned with its business objectives. A practical tip for implementation is to conduct periodic workshops with relevant stakeholders to gather insights and recalibrate the scoring system, fostering a culture of risk awareness throughout the organization.

6.2: Risk Matrix Utilization

Risk matrices serve as powerful visual tools that can clearly illustrate the potential risks faced by an organization and help prioritize those risks based on their severity and likelihood. By plotting risks on a matrix that displays both their impact and probability, cyber security professionals can quickly see which risks demand immediate attention and resources. This visual representation simplifies complex risk data, making it easier to communicate the necessity for action to stakeholders who may not have a technical background. Colour coding often enhances these matrices, with different colours indicating varying levels of risk, facilitating faster understanding and more effective discussions during risk management meetings.

For constructing an effective risk matrix, several best practices should be observed. First, clearly define the criteria for risk levels, ensuring everyone involved understands the terms like 'impact' and 'probability.' Consistency in rating these dimensions is crucial, so adopting a common scale or using qualitative descriptions can help maintain uniformity across different assessments. It is also essential to engage diverse perspectives—drawing insights from various teams can provide a more comprehensive view of the risks at hand. Updating the matrix regularly to reflect new data or changes in the environment is vital for relevance. Lastly, remember that a risk matrix is a living document; use it as a dynamic tool rather than a static report, continuously revisiting and refining it to adapt to evolving threats in the cyber landscape.

To enhance the utility of your risk matrix, consider using accompanying tools or software that can automate parts of the process, especially in data gathering and analysis. Integration with existing risk management frameworks will enable a holistic approach, supporting informed decision-making throughout the organization. Taking these steps not only improves the effectiveness of the risk matrix but also reinforces a culture of proactive risk management.

6.3: Top Risks Determination

A systematic process for identifying an organization's top risks begins with thorough data gathering, involving both qualitative and quantitative analysis. Understanding the organization's context is crucial, which includes its mission, objectives, and the industry landscape. Engaging with various stakeholders, including IT, operations, and senior management, can provide diverse perspectives on potential vulnerabilities and threats. Once the data is collected, risk assessments should utilize frameworks like NIST, ISO 31000, or FAIR to quantify risks based on their likelihood and impact.

After risks are identified, they must be prioritized. This priority ranking should consider both the severity of potential impacts on the organization and the likelihood of occurrence. Utilizing a risk matrix can aid in visualizing these priorities, helping teams focus attention on the most pressing issues. Regularly revisiting and updating the risk identification process ensures that new threats are acknowledged, especially as technology and the threat landscape evolve rapidly.

The identification of top risks significantly impacts resource allocation decisions. Organizations tend to allocate resources to those areas that pose the highest risks, ensuring the protection of critical assets and maintaining compliance with regulations. By aligning budgetary decisions with identified risks, security teams can create targeted strategies that address vulnerabilities effectively. This alignment also facilitates the development of business cases for investments in security initiatives, demonstrating to leadership how proactive measures can mitigate risks and enhance the organization's resilience. It's important to continually measure the effectiveness of such resource allocations and adjust strategies as necessary to respond to the dynamic nature of cyber threats.

When assessing risks, a practical tip is to engage in scenario planning. By envisioning various threat scenarios, organizations can better prepare for unexpected incidents, refining their risk management strategies and ensuring sufficient resources are set aside for rapid response and recovery efforts.

Chapter 7: Risk Mitigation Techniques

7.1: Security Controls Implementation

Security controls serve as the backbone of any robust risk management strategy in cybersecurity. They can be categorized broadly into three types: administrative, technical, and physical controls. Administrative controls encompass policies and procedures, encompassing training programs that establish guidelines for cybersecurity best practices among employees. Technical controls leverage technology to protect systems and data, such as firewalls, intrusion detection systems, and encryption protocols. Physical controls focus on protecting the physical infrastructure, including locks, surveillance cameras, and secure access points to prevent unauthorized physical access to sensitive areas. Implementing a combination of these controls can effectively mitigate a wide range of risks, as they address both human behaviour and technological vulnerabilities.

The effectiveness of combining different types of controls is pivotal in establishing a layered security approach, often described in cybersecurity as defense in depth. By integrating administrative, technical, and physical controls, organizations create multiple barriers that an attacker must breach to compromise a system effectively. For instance, while a firewall can block unauthorized access, proper training can mitigate the risk of social engineering attacks that bypass technical defenses. Similarly, combining threat detection technologies with physical security ensures that breaches are detected early, and access to critical areas is limited. This layered approach not only increases the overall security posture but also provides resilience; if one control fails, others continue to provide protection. Consequently, organizations should regularly evaluate and update their security measures, ensuring that they adapt to evolving threats and maintain an effective security environment.

Understanding that no single control is infallible is crucial in risk management. It's imperative for cybersecurity professionals to assess the unique risk landscape of their organization continually. This involves not only implementing a variety of security controls but also testing and refining them regularly through simulations and audits. A valuable practice is to conduct tabletop exercises that involve various departments, thereby revealing gaps in the controls that may not be visible from a purely technical perspective. By fostering a culture of collaboration and vigilance in security practices, organizations can better prepare themselves against potential threats and enhance their overall risk management strategies.

7.2: Incident Response Planning

An effective incident response plan is built on several critical elements that work together to mitigate risks and respond to threats efficiently. First and foremost, the plan should include a clear definition of roles and responsibilities among team members. Each individual must understand their specific duties in the event of an incident. This clarity helps eliminate confusion during high-pressure situations. Communication protocols are another vital component; establishing how information will flow among team members and stakeholders is essential for a coordinated response. Furthermore, incorporating policies for threat detection and assessment will enable the team to identify incidents promptly and classify them based on severity. The plan must also outline procedures for containment, eradication, and recovery, ensuring that the organization can restore normal operations as swiftly as possible. Additionally, regular updates and revisions to the incident response plan are crucial in adapting to the evolving threat landscape and organizational changes.

Training and drills play a pivotal role in enhancing an organization's incident response readiness. Even the most meticulously crafted plan can fall short if the team lacks practical experience. Conducting regular training sessions ensures that staff are familiar with the procedures outlined in the incident response plan. This familiarity enhances their confidence and helps them react swiftly when a real incident occurs. Drills simulate various types of incidents, providing an opportunity to test the effectiveness of the response plan and identify any gaps that need addressing. During these exercises, participants can practice their roles in a controlled environment, refining their skills and honing their decision-making abilities. Such preparedness not only equips the team to handle potential threats but also fosters a culture of awareness and vigilance throughout the organization.

Ultimately, a well-thought-out incident response plan and ongoing training initiatives create a robust cybersecurity posture. Emphasizing the importance of both elements empowers cybersecurity professionals to manage risks effectively and respond to incidents with authority. A practical tip for maintaining readiness is to schedule periodic reviews of both the incident response plan and training sessions. This proactive approach ensures that the team stays informed of the latest threat vectors and response techniques, further solidifying their capability to protect the organization's assets.

7.3: Layered Defense Strategies

Layered defense, often referred to as a defense-in-depth approach, is a fundamental cybersecurity strategy that emphasizes multiple protective measures at various levels. This concept is significant because it acknowledges that no single security control is foolproof. By implementing a multitude of defenses, organizations can effectively reduce vulnerabilities and strengthen their overall security posture. The idea is to create a comprehensive barrier that can detect, deter, and respond to threats in real-time, ensuring that even if one layer fails, others will still provide protection. This multifaceted approach is critical in today's dynamic cyber environment, where threats are constantly evolving and becoming more sophisticated.

The layers of defense in a cybersecurity strategy typically include physical security, network security, endpoint security, application security, data protection, and user awareness training. Each layer plays a distinct role but is interconnected with the others, creating a robust security ecosystem. For instance, physical security safeguards the hardware and infrastructure, while network security protects data in transit. Endpoint security focuses on individual devices, ensuring they are secure against malware and unauthorized access. Application security addresses vulnerabilities within software applications, and data protection measures secure sensitive information from breaches. Lastly, user awareness training empowers employees to recognize and respond to potential threats, acting as the last line of defense. The interplay among these layers forms a cohesive strategy that significantly enhances resilience against attacks.

A solid layered defense strategy not only involves implementing various security measures but also ensuring they work in harmony. Regular assessments and updates are essential to adapt to emerging threats. Organizations should prioritize integration and collaboration among security solutions, such as employing advanced threat detection tools that communicate across layers. This integrated approach allows for real-time incident response and better overall situational awareness. As you refine your layered defense strategy, consider performing regular security drills and simulations to evaluate the performance of each layer and ensure that all employees are prepared for incidents. Such proactive initiatives foster a culture of security awareness, making your organization not just responsive but also resilient in the face of cybersecurity challenges.

Chapter 8: Risk Acceptance and Transfer

8.1: Defining Risk Tolerance Levels

Risk tolerance is a crucial concept in the realm of cyber security and organizational decision-making. It refers to the degree of variability in outcomes that an organization is willing to accept in pursuit of its objectives. Understanding and defining risk tolerance is vital because it informs how an organization responds to threats, prioritizes resource allocation, and executes its overall security strategy. A well-articulated risk tolerance helps organizations navigate the cyber landscape effectively, allowing them to balance between risk and reward while protecting their assets and ensuring compliance with relevant regulations. This understanding should permeate through all levels of the organization, guiding teams in making informed decisions regarding security practices and investments.

To effectively define and communicate risk tolerance across teams, organizations can adopt various methodologies. One effective approach is to engage in collaborative workshops where stakeholders from different departments come together to delineate their perspectives on risk. This can involve scenario-based exercises that help quantify potential risks and their impacts, fostering a shared understanding among team members. Furthermore, utilizing visual aids, such as risk matrices or dashboards, can enhance communication by providing tangible representations of risk levels and thresholds. Regular training sessions and updates on evolving threats can also help maintain alignment on risk tolerance, ensuring that all teams remain aware of organizational priorities and can adjust their operations accordingly.

Establishing a clear definition of risk tolerance is not an event but rather an ongoing process. Organizations should continuously assess and evaluate their risk tolerance in light of changing environments and emerging threats. Engaging in regular discussions and reviews of previous decisions and their outcomes will help refine the understanding of risk tolerance over time. Cyber security professionals should not only focus on defining risk tolerance but also strive to cultivate a culture of risk awareness within their teams. Encouraging open dialogue about risks, sharing lessons learned, and acknowledging that every member plays a role in managing risk can lead to a more cohesive and proactive approach to cyber security.

8.2: Insurance as a Risk Transfer Strategy

Insurance offers a structured approach to transferring specific risks that organizations encounter, particularly in the realm of cybersecurity. Companies invest in insurance policies as a means to mitigate potential financial losses stemming from data breaches, cyber-attacks, and various operational disruptions. By paying a premium, organizations can shift the burden of covering certain losses to the insurer, allowing them to focus on managing and mitigating risks on other fronts. Cyber insurance policies are specifically tailored to address the unique challenges of the digital landscape, often covering costs associated with data recovery, legal fees, and public relations efforts needed to manage the fallout from a cyber incident. This risk transfer mechanism is especially vital for businesses that may lack the financial resources to recover from substantial breaches, as it enables them to maintain financial stability while continuing to invest in security measures.

Despite its advantages, there are significant limitations and considerations in relying on insurance as a risk management strategy. One primary concern is the complexity of understanding the coverage terms and exclusions common to cyber insurance policies. Many organizations may find themselves underinsured due to non-compliance with specific policy requirements or misunderstandings about what their policy truly covers, especially when faced with a cyber incident. Additionally, the cost of premiums can escalate based on an organization's risk profile, leading to challenges in budget allocation for cybersecurity initiatives. Insurers are increasingly requiring organizations to demonstrate robust cybersecurity practices before issuing or renewing a policy, which demands a comprehensive risk management approach. Furthermore, insurance should not be seen as a substitute for proactive risk management practices; rather, it should complement a holistic strategy that includes risk assessment, mitigation, and continuous improvement of cyber defenses.

Cybersecurity professionals should be proactive in evaluating their risk transfer options. Engaging with insurance providers to clarify coverage details, understanding policy limitations, and regularly updating risk assessments in light of evolving threats is crucial. Identifying key risks that can be effectively transferred can help in crafting a comprehensive risk management strategy. Investing time in enhancing the organization's overall cybersecurity posture not only makes it more insurable, but also significantly reduces the risk of incidents occurring in the first place. Balancing risk avoidance, acceptance, mitigation, and transfer will create a more resilient organization in the ever-evolving cyber threat landscape.

8.3: Outsourcing and Third-Party Risks

Engaging third-party vendors for security functions introduces a range of significant risks that organizations must navigate carefully. The reliance on external partners opens up avenues for vulnerabilities that may not be immediately visible. When organizations outsource critical security responsibilities, they entrust sensitive data, infrastructure, and compliance requirements to external parties who might not adhere to the same rigorous standards as the primary organization. These risks include potential data breaches, lack of transparency in operations, and inadequate incident response capabilities. Moreover, third-party vendors may have access to a company's systems, creating potential entry points for attackers. If these vendors suffer a security incident or fail to meet their security obligations, the primary organization may face substantial repercussions, including financial losses and reputational damage.

To mitigate these risks, organizations must implement a comprehensive vetting process for all prospective third-party vendors. This involves not only assessing the vendor's security practices and history but also demanding transparency in their operations and compliance with recognized security standards. Contract management plays a crucial role here; having well-drafted agreements that stipulate security expectations, responsibilities, and accountability can protect the organization significantly. Regular reviews and audits of vendor performance against these contractual obligations should be standard practice. It's important to ensure that vendors also have a robust incident response plan and a proven track record in managing security threats. This disciplined approach reinforces a culture of security awareness and accountability, which is essential in today's digital landscape.

The effective management of third-party risks hinges on both vigilance and proactive measures. Organizations should instil a continuous risk assessment framework that is updated regularly to reflect changing risks, technologies, and vendor landscapes. Leveraging tools for ongoing monitoring of vendor security compliance can provide insights and early warnings about potential vulnerabilities. Training internal teams to identify potential red flags and communicate with third-party partners effectively enhances the overall security posture. These practices are essential not only to safeguard critical assets but also to build resilience against an ever-evolving threat landscape, ensuring that outsourcing decisions contribute positively to the organization's security goals.

Chapter 9: Monitoring and Reviewing Risks

9.1: Continuous Risk Monitoring Techniques

Continuous monitoring techniques play a crucial role in maintaining an organization's awareness of its risk levels, providing a proactive approach to risk management. The dynamic nature of cyber threats necessitates a shift from traditional, periodic assessments to real-time monitoring that can swiftly identify emerging vulnerabilities and threats. Using continuous monitoring allows organizations to have a constant pulse on their security posture, making it easier to detect anomalies, track compliance status, and make informed decisions quickly. This approach integrates various data sources, including system logs, network traffic, and user behaviour patterns, thereby enhancing the visibility and understanding of potential risks. By incorporating automation tools and advanced analytics, professionals can streamline the monitoring process, allowing for quicker responses to incidents and more efficient resource allocation.

There are several tools and technologies available that assist in effective risk monitoring, transforming the way cyber security professionals manage threats. Security Information and Event Management (SIEM) solutions aggregate and analyze security data from across the environment, enabling real-time visibility into incidents and alerts. Other tools, such as intrusion detection systems (IDS) and network monitoring solutions, complement SIEM by providing critical insights into network traffic and suspicious activities. Additionally, vulnerability management tools continuously scan and assess systems for flaws, ensuring that organizations stay updated on potential exposures. Cloud-based security solutions also offer scalable monitoring capabilities, allowing for quick adjustments as the threat landscape evolves. These technologies often incorporate machine learning algorithms to enhance detection capabilities, enabling organizations to stay one step ahead of attackers.

9.2: Metrics and Key Performance Indicators

To measure the effectiveness of risk management efforts in cybersecurity, it is essential to identify key metrics and performance indicators. These metrics serve as valuable tools for evaluating how well an organization is managing its risks. Commonly used metrics include the number of identified vulnerabilities, the time taken to remediate those vulnerabilities, and the frequency of security incidents. Other important KPIs might involve the impact of security breaches on business operations and the effectiveness of communication in risk awareness among employees. By focusing on these metrics, cybersecurity professionals can gain insight into their organization's risk posture and make informed decisions about where to allocate resources and improve their security strategies.

Establishing baselines for these KPIs is a critical step in effective risk management. A baseline provides a reference point against which future performance can be measured. To create an accurate baseline, collect historical data on relevant metrics so that trends can be analyzed over time. This involves determining average values, variations, and any significant outliers that may skew the data. Once a reliable baseline is in place, organizations can utilize this data to track improvements or declines in risk management performance, thereby facilitating informed decision-making. Regularly reviewing these baselines allows cybersecurity professionals to adjust their tactics and priorities based on real-world performance and shifts in risk landscapes.

Continuously monitoring metrics and KPIs not only enhances awareness of security effectiveness but also aids in identifying areas for improvement. Not all security efforts yield immediate visible results; therefore, interpreting these indicators wisely is crucial. Engaging stakeholders by sharing metric trends can foster a culture of security within the organization and inspire collective accountability. As organizations adapt their risk management strategies based on empirical data, they should remember that metrics should be relevant and connected to their risk appetite and overall business goals. Investing time in refining these measures will ultimately lead to a more resilient cybersecurity posture.

9.3: Conducting Regular Risk Reviews

Regular risk reviews are crucial in the ever-evolving landscape of cybersecurity threats. As organizations grow and technology advances, the risks they face change simultaneously. Factors such as new vulnerabilities, evolving attack techniques, and changing regulatory requirements necessitate ongoing scrutiny. Conducting these reviews allows teams to identify potential risks early, adapt their security strategies accordingly, and prioritize resources effectively. With a proactive approach, teams can better guard against unforeseen incidents, ensuring organizational resilience and maintaining trust with stakeholders.

To conduct effective risk review sessions within teams, a structured framework can help streamline the process and enhance outcomes. Start by assembling a diverse group of stakeholders, including IT, compliance, and operational personnel, ensuring multiple perspectives are considered. Define the objectives of the review—whether it's assessing current controls, identifying emerging threats, or examining past incidents. Use a systematic approach to outline the specific risks under consideration, allowing the team to assess their likelihood and potential impact critically. Encourage open dialogue and brainstorming sessions, ensuring everyone's voice is heard. Finally, document findings and action items clearly to facilitate accountability and follow-up. Regularly scheduled reviews, whether quarterly or biannually, can help maintain momentum and reinforce a culture of vigilance across the organization.

As a practical tip, consider incorporating threat intelligence into your review sessions. By analyzing emerging threats and correlating them with your current risk profile, your team can better prioritize which risks to address first, ensuring that your defenses remain robust against the most pertinent threats. This proactive incorporation of intelligence can significantly enhance the effectiveness of your risk management strategy.

Chapter 10: Compliance and Legal Considerations

10.1: Regulatory Requirements Overview

Regulatory requirements surrounding cybersecurity are critical across various industries, shaping how organizations protect their digital assets and information. Laws and standards such as the General Data Protection Regulation (GDPR) in Europe, the Health Insurance Portability and Accountability Act (HIPAA) in the United States, and the Payment Card Industry Data Security Standard (PCI DSS), have set benchmarks for data protection. These regulations mandate companies to implement robust security measures, conduct regular audits, and report data breaches within specified timeframes. Industries like finance, healthcare, and retail are particularly affected, as the data they handle is sensitive and requires stringent safeguards. Compliance with these regulations is not merely a formality; it signifies an organization's commitment to protecting customer information, enhancing trust, and ensuring operational resilience against cyber threats.

The implications of compliance extend deeply into the realm of risk management strategies. Organizations must develop risk management frameworks that not only meet regulatory standards but also align with their overall business objectives. This requires a proactive approach where risk assessments are performed to identify potential vulnerabilities and threats. By integrating compliance into their risk management processes, organizations can prioritize their security investments, ensuring that resources are allocated effectively where they are most needed. Furthermore, compliance drives the creation of incident response plans and training programs that prepare teams to act swiftly and effectively in the event of a security breach. Regulatory adherence fosters a culture of security, prompting continuous improvement and evaluation of cyber defense mechanisms.

Understanding the nuances of regulatory requirements and their impact on risk management is essential for cybersecurity professionals. Staying informed about changes in laws and standards can provide a competitive edge, allowing organizations to anticipate compliance challenges and adapt their strategies accordingly. Engaging in ongoing education and leveraging resources offered by regulatory bodies can significantly enhance an organization's capability to manage cyber risks effectively. This proactive stance not only aids in maintaining compliance but also cultivates resilience against evolving cyber threats.

10.2: Data Protection and Privacy Laws

Understanding the landscape of data protection and privacy laws is crucial for cyber security professionals engaged in risk management. Two of the most prominent regulations in this domain are the General Data Protection Regulation (GDPR) and the California Consumer Privacy Act (CCPA). The GDPR, which came into effect in May 2018, sets a high standard for privacy and data protection in the European Union. It emphasizes the rights of individuals, giving them more control over their personal data, and necessitates that organizations implement stringent measures to protect that data. Key elements of GDPR include mandatory data breach notifications, data protection impact assessments, and the appointment of Data Protection Officers in certain circumstances. Similarly, the CCPA, which became effective in January 2020, grants California residents specific rights regarding their personal information, including the right to know what data is being collected, the right to delete personal information, and the right to opt out of the sale of their data. Both regulations reflect a broader global trend toward increased accountability and transparency in data handling practices.

Aligning risk management with compliance obligations requires practical strategies that address the unique challenges posed by these regulations. Organizations need to conduct thorough audits of their data processing activities to identify potential gaps in compliance with GDPR and CCPA requirements. This involves not just understanding the data they collect but also mapping out the data lifecycle — from collection and storage to usage and deletion. Implementing robust data governance frameworks is essential to ensure that data handling practices meet legal standards. Leveraging automated tools for monitoring data access, tracking data flows, and managing consent can significantly streamline compliance efforts. Additionally, employee training is vital; ensuring that all staff members understand their responsibilities under these laws can minimize risks stemming from human error. Integrating risk management with privacy by design practices enhances an organization's resilience against data breaches and fosters customer trust.

Staying updated on evolving data protection regulations is imperative for cyber security professionals. As laws continue to change and new regulations emerge, investing in ongoing education and training will help teams remain compliant while effectively managing risks. Building a culture of privacy and security within the organization not only aligns risk management strategies with compliance efforts but also positions the business as a leader in ethical data usage. This proactive approach ensures that organizations not only meet legal obligations but also reinforce their commitment to protecting user privacy in an increasingly digital world. Regularly reviewing and updating data protection strategies will keep your practice relevant and resilient in the face of new challenges.

10.3: Consequences of Non-Compliance

Failure to comply with regulatory standards and industry best practices can lead to severe financial penalties, potential legal actions, and lasting damage to a company's reputation. Organizations that neglect compliance risk incurring hefty fines, which may escalate depending on the severity and duration of the violation. These fines can significantly impact a company's financial health, diverting vital resources away from innovation and growth. Moreover, non-compliance can provoke legal actions from regulatory bodies or other stakeholders, resulting in costly litigations. Such disputes not only drain financial resources but can also lead to lengthy court battles that demand attention away from core business operations. The reputational damage that accompanies non-compliance can be just as damaging as the financial repercussions; loss of customer trust and negative media exposure can linger, making it difficult for organizations to regain their standing in the market.

Maintaining a proactive approach to compliance is crucial for organizations striving to mitigate these risks. By integrating compliance into the organization's culture, professionals can create an environment where adherence to regulations is prioritized. Regular training, continuous monitoring, and adopting compliance technology can all contribute to a robust compliance framework. This proactive stance not only helps in identifying compliance gaps before they can escalate into serious issues but also fosters a culture of accountability within the organization. Engaging with regulatory changes in advance allows companies to prepare and implement necessary adjustments swiftly, ensuring they are equipped to meet evolving requirements and reduce the chance of facing fines or lawsuits. Emphasizing proactive compliance ultimately serves as a safeguard against the risks associated with non-compliance, securing both the organization's future and its stakeholders' interests.

For cyber security professionals, staying informed about the latest compliance requirements and changes in legislation is vital. Regular brainstorming sessions and interdepartmental collaborations can facilitate a unified approach toward compliance. Establishing a designated compliance team might also prove beneficial for monitoring regulations, ensuring that the organization remains not just compliant but also a step ahead in the ever-evolving landscape of cyber security.

Chapter 11: Risk Communication and Reporting

11.1: Stakeholder Identification and Engagement

Identifying stakeholders is a critical first step in effective risk management, especially in the fast-evolving realm of cyber security. Stakeholders include everyone who has an interest in the risks that an organization faces, such as employees, clients, shareholders, regulatory bodies, and even the broader community. Understanding who these stakeholders are helps cyber security professionals recognize differing perspectives and priorities regarding risk. These individuals or groups may perceive risks differently based on their unique positions within or outside the organization. For example, while the IT department may be primarily focused on technical vulnerabilities, upper management may be more concerned with financial implications and regulatory compliance. Hence, taking the time to identify stakeholders ensures that a broad range of viewpoints and insights can be considered during the risk assessment process, leading to more comprehensive and robust risk management plans.

When it comes to engaging stakeholders in risk communication, clarity and consistency are paramount. Effective engagement begins with establishing open lines of communication that allow for regular interaction and feedback. Cyber security professionals should employ tailored communication strategies that resonate with different stakeholders, as each group may require a distinct approach. For instance, technical discussions about cyber threats may be appropriate for IT staff but need to be simplified for non-technical stakeholders. Regular workshops, webinars, and briefings can facilitate dialogue and help stakeholders feel included in the risk management process. Empowering them with knowledge not only builds trust but also enhances their ability to contribute to risk mitigation strategies. Additionally, utilizing tools such as surveys or stakeholder interviews can provide valuable insights into their concerns and expectations, helping to align risk management efforts with stakeholder interests.

Remember that stakeholder engagement is an ongoing process that necessitates continuous assessment and adaptation. Technologies and threat landscapes are constantly changing, which means that effective risk management must remain dynamic. Encourage stakeholders to participate actively by seeking their input not just during formal meetings but throughout the risk management life cycle. This approach not only strengthens relationships but also fosters a culture of security awareness across the organization. A practical tip is to develop a stakeholder map and prioritize interactions based on their influence and interest in cyber security risks. Keeping stakeholders informed and engaged transforms them from passive observers into active participants, enhancing the overall resilience of the organization against cyber threats.

11.2: Effective Risk Reporting Practices

Creating clear and concise risk reports is vital for effective communication among various audiences in the realm of cyber security. To achieve this, one must first identify the audience for each report, tailoring the language and depth of information to suit their context. For technical teams, detailed insights into vulnerabilities, threat vectors, and mitigation strategies are necessary. On the other hand, executive summaries should focus on high-level risks, potential impacts on business objectives, and strategic recommendations, avoiding jargon that may confuse or alienate non-technical stakeholders. Visual aids such as graphs and charts can effectively convey complex data, engaging readers and allowing them to grasp critical information at a glance. Additionally, maintaining a consistent format across reports helps in establishing a standard that readers can easily navigate, making the information more accessible and actionable.

Context and relevance play crucial roles in risk reporting and must not be overlooked. Reports should frame risks within the specific environment of the organization, considering factors such as recent incidents, industry trends, and emerging threats that could impact operations. Providing background information on incidents, like the severity and frequency of similar breaches in the industry, can highlight the urgency of addressing identified risks. Furthermore, it's important to link risks to business objectives, demonstrating how unaddressed vulnerabilities could hinder achieving strategic goals. The more relevant the information, the more likely it is to drive action and engage stakeholders in risk management. Stakeholders will be more inclined to act if they understand not just the 'what' of the risks, but also the 'why' behind prioritizing certain actions.

By focusing on clarity and relevance, risk reporting can transform from mere compliance documents into powerful management tools. It's beneficial to incorporate feedback after report distributions, refining future reports based on what worked and what didn't. Engage with readers to understand their perspectives and needs better, and continually adapt reporting practices. This iterative approach leads to more effective risk management across the organization, making sure that everyone is informed and aligned in safeguarding against cyber threats.

11.3: Communicating Risk to Non-technical Audiences

Translating complex risk concepts into language that non-technical stakeholders can grasp involves the use of relatable analogies, clear visuals, and straightforward terminology. Cybersecurity professionals must think about their audience's perspective and acknowledge that terms like 'malware' or 'phishing' may not hold the same weight for them as they do within technical circles. Instead of diving deep into jargon, consider using simple illustrations—such as comparing cybersecurity risks to familiar concepts like insurance, where the idea is to protect against potential loss. This technique helps in framing risk in a context that is easily understandable. Using charts or infographics can aid in visually representing the likelihood of various threats, thus making the information more digestible. It is also beneficial to share real-world examples, as these can evoke a stronger emotional response and highlight the potential impact of risks on the organization or individual in a direct manner.

Effective communication of risk plays a pivotal role in enhancing decision-making processes. When stakeholders comprehend the risks presented to them, they are better equipped to make informed choices that affect their organization. For instance, when technical teams translate security vulnerabilities into potential business impacts, decision-makers can prioritize actions based on factors such as financial implications or reputational damage. A well-informed leader is more likely to allocate resources effectively and dedicate time to preventative measures. Clear communication fosters a sense of shared responsibility, which encourages collaboration between technical and non-technical teams. Stakeholders who understand the rationale behind risk management strategies are more inclined to support initiatives aimed at mitigating those risks. This alignment is crucial for creating a culture of security awareness within an organization.

A practical tip for cybersecurity professionals is to develop a 'risk communication toolkit' that includes templates for reports and presentations in a format suitable for non-technical audiences. This toolkit can help streamline the translation of complex information into clear, actionable insights. Regular training sessions that involve role-playing scenarios can further enhance skills in articulating risks to diverse audiences. By honing these skills, cybersecurity professionals can ensure that critical risk information reaches those who need it, ultimately strengthening the organization's overall posture towards cybersecurity.

Chapter 12: Cyber Security Governance

12.1: Establishing a Governance Framework

A robust cybersecurity governance framework is built on several essential components. First and foremost is the establishment of a clear set of policies and objectives that define the organization's approach to cybersecurity. These policies should align with the overall business goals and ensure compliance with relevant regulations and standards. Another critical component is the identification and allocation of resources, including personnel, technology, and funding, necessary to support the framework. This involves not only hiring skilled professionals but also providing ongoing training to keep teams updated on the latest threats and best practices. Additionally, a robust framework incorporates mechanisms for continual monitoring and assessment. This includes regular audits of existing security measures and updates to policies in response to emerging threats. Finally, effective communication and reporting processes ensure that all stakeholders, from executive leadership to operational staff, are aware of their roles and responsibilities within the cybersecurity landscape.

To support effective risk management, a well-defined governance structure is essential. This should begin with creating a cybersecurity steering committee comprised of key stakeholders from various departments, including IT, finance, legal, and operations. This committee is responsible for overseeing the implementation of the governance framework and ensuring that risk management practices are consistently applied across the organization. Establishing clear lines of authority and accountability is vital, as this ensures that everyone understands who is responsible for various aspects of cybersecurity. Alongside this, developing a risk appetite statement will guide decision-making by clarifying how much risk the organization is willing to accept to pursue its objectives. Furthermore, integrating risk management into everyday business processes fosters a culture of security where every employee recognizes their role in mitigating risks. Regular reporting and updates to executive leadership keep them informed and engaged, supporting a top-down approach to governance that emphasizes the importance of cybersecurity as a critical business function.

For practical implementation, organizations should periodically revisit their governance framework and risk management strategies to adapt to changing circumstances. Cyber threats evolve rapidly, and the governance framework must be agile enough to respond to new challenges. Regular training sessions and simulations can help prepare teams for potential incidents, enhancing their response readiness. Always remember that successful governance is not a one-time event but an ongoing commitment to foster a secure environment for your organization.

12.2: Roles and Responsibilities in Risk Management

Understanding the roles and responsibilities of various stakeholders within the risk management process is paramount for the success of any cybersecurity initiative. Each stakeholder, from executive leadership to individual team members, plays a crucial part in identifying, assessing, and mitigating risks. Management is responsible for establishing the overall risk governance framework and providing necessary resources. They must ensure that risk management is prioritized within the organization. Cybersecurity teams are charged with implementing security measures, continuously monitoring potential threats, and responding to incidents. Additionally, end-users play a vital role by adhering to security protocols and reporting unusual activities. Clear communication between these parties fosters a collaborative environment where risk management is viewed as a shared responsibility rather than a siloed function. This collective approach enhances the organization's ability to navigate risks effectively.

Clear accountability is essential for improving risk management outcomes and ensuring that all stakeholders understand their roles and the expectations placed upon them. When accountability is defined, it leads to better ownership of tasks and responsibilities, which enhances response times and the overall efficiency of risk management efforts. It empowers stakeholders to not only fulfill their immediate roles but also encourages them to proactively identify potential risks and suggest improvements. Organizations with clear lines of accountability are more likely to succeed in their risk management strategies, as there is a culture of responsiveness and vigilance. Regular reviews and updates of roles and responsibilities can reinforce this accountability, aligning teams with the changing landscape of threats and vulnerabilities. Teams that feel a sense of ownership over their responsibilities are often more engaged and invested in the risk management process.

Effective risk management is amplified when organizations foster a culture of transparency and collaboration among stakeholders. Establishing a common language regarding risks and the corresponding responsibilities enables more effective communication and reduces misunderstandings. Consider integrating risk management training into regular professional development programs to prepare staff at all levels. Empowering employees with the knowledge of their roles in risk management not only strengthens the organization's defense mechanisms but also cultivates an environment where risk awareness is embedded in the corporate culture. This proactive alignment of roles and responsibilities supports the organization's resilience against cyber threats.

12.3: Governance Processes and Policies

Governance processes are essential for effective oversight and control of cybersecurity initiatives. They provide a structured approach to managing risks while ensuring compliance with organizational objectives and regulatory standards. A well-defined governance framework not only clarifies roles and responsibilities but also fosters accountability across all levels of an organization. Within this framework, risk assessments, audits, and performance metrics play critical roles in evaluating the effectiveness of cybersecurity strategies. By integrating these processes, organizations can better anticipate potential threats, enabling them to make informed decisions that enhance their overall security posture.

Policies must be formulated to align with governance objectives and address regulatory requirements. These policies serve as guiding principles that inform daily operations and strategic direction in cybersecurity. Effective policies can dictate everything from incident response protocols to data protection standards and employee conduct regarding sensitive information. Ensuring these policies remain dynamic and adaptable is vital; they should evolve in response to changing technologies and risk landscapes. Regular training and awareness programs are essential to ensure that all employees understand and adhere to these policies, creating a culture of security awareness throughout the organization.

Implementing a strong governance framework alongside comprehensive policies leads to a cohesive risk management strategy. Cybersecurity professionals should continuously evaluate their governance processes and policies to ensure they are not only meeting current compliance requirements but also proactively addressing emerging threats. This iterative approach helps in refining security measures and ensuring that organizations remain resilient against potential cyber incidents.

Chapter 13: Incident Management and Response

13.1: Creating an Incident Response Plan

An effective incident response plan is crucial for organizations aiming to mitigate potential threats and respond swiftly to cyber incidents. At the foundation of such a plan are critical elements that should not be overlooked. First, establishing a clear communication strategy is vital. This includes identifying key stakeholders, determining the flow of information, and ensuring that communication channels remain secure yet accessible during incidents. Furthermore, organizations must define roles and responsibilities to ensure that team members know their specific tasks during an incident. This fosters accountability and speeds up response times.

Another important element is the development of detailed incident detection and analysis procedures. Organizations need to have the right tools and technologies in place to detect incidents as they occur. Along with this, proper training for the incident response team is necessary to ensure that they can accurately assess incidents and understand their implications for the organization. Additionally, maintaining an incident log can help track the timeline of events and actions taken, providing invaluable information for after-action reviews.

Integrating incident response planning with risk management is essential to create a holistic security posture within an organization. Risk management identifies potential threats and vulnerabilities, which creates a foundation for the incident response plan. By conducting a thorough risk assessment, organizations can highlight the most critical assets to protect, which in turn helps prioritize incident response efforts. This integration ensures that the organization is not only prepared to respond to incidents but also actively working to minimize the risks and impact of such events. Regular reviews of the incident response plan should coincide with risk management evaluations, allowing for updates based on emerging threats or changes in organizational structure.

One practical tip is to conduct regular tabletop exercises that simulate incidents. These exercises not only test the incident response plan but also enhance collaboration between the incident response team and risk management. As threats continually evolve, fostering an environment of practice and adaptability is crucial for an effective incident response strategy.

13.2: Post-Incident Analysis and Review

Conducting thorough post-incident analyses is crucial for any organization aiming to improve its cyber security posture. These analyses allow teams to dissect incidents, uncover weaknesses, and identify what went wrong. By understanding the root causes of incidents, organizations can implement changes that not only mitigate similar risks in the future but also enhance overall resilience. Each incident offers valuable lessons; however, without dedicated and systematic reviews, these insights can be lost. A culture that prioritizes learning from past events fosters a proactive approach to risk management, enabling teams to stay one step ahead of potential threats.

To effectively document lessons learned, organizations should establish a framework that guides the post-incident review process. This framework should include key elements, such as incident timelines, involved parties, response efforts, and outcomes. Furthermore, incorporating feedback from all stakeholders enhances the analysis and provides diverse perspectives on what occurred. Regularly scheduled reviews of these documented lessons can create a repository of knowledge that informs future risk assessments and response strategies. By leveraging this information, teams can not only avoid repeating past mistakes but also refine their incident response plans and strengthen organizational defenses.

A practical tip for improving post-incident analyses is to integrate a retrospective approach that encourages open dialogue and honest assessments. During reviews, emphasize the importance of creating a safe environment where team members feel comfortable sharing their insights without fear of blame. This openness leads to richer discussions and more meaningful takeaways, ultimately driving continuous improvement and reinforcing a culture of accountability within the organization.

13.3: Legal Implications of Incident Response

Legal considerations are critical in every aspect of incident response. Organizations must navigate a complex web of laws and regulations that govern data breaches, privacy, and notification requirements. These legal obligations can vary significantly depending on the industry, the geographical location of the organization, and the type of data involved. For example, personal data protection laws such as the General Data Protection Regulation (GDPR) in Europe impose strict requirements for reporting incidents that may affect individuals' data rights. Companies must be aware of their obligations not just to their customers but also to regulatory bodies, which may require them to disclose incidents within specified time frames. Failing to comply with these legal obligations can result in hefty fines, lawsuits, and reputational damage, making it essential for Incident Response Teams (IRTs) to be well-versed in the legal landscape related to cybersecurity incidents.

The incident management process should always incorporate legal consultation as a standard practice. Engaging legal counsel during an incident can provide essential guidance on how to proceed without compromising the organization's legal standing. Legal advisors can help interpret applicable laws, ensure compliance with notification requirements, and evaluate the possible legal ramifications of various response strategies. Additionally, they can assist in crafting communication plans that accurately convey necessary information without exposing the organization to liability, such as making vague or misleading statements. Legal professionals can also guide an organization in understanding when to engage law enforcement authorities or report incidents to regulatory agencies, ensuring that all actions taken align with legal obligations. This collaboration between cybersecurity professionals and legal experts is crucial in managing incidents effectively while minimizing future risks.

Integrating legal considerations into the incident response strategy enhances overall cybersecurity risk management. Regular legal reviews and updates to the incident response plan should be conducted to account for any changes in regulations or case law. Cybersecurity professionals must stay informed about evolving legal standards, particularly in jurisdictions relevant to their operations. Within this context, a proactive approach toward legal implications can safeguard the organization against legal pitfalls while fortifying its incident response framework.

Chapter 14: Future Trends in Cyber Security Risk Management

14.1: Machine Learning and AI in Risk Management

Machine learning and artificial intelligence are revolutionizing the way organizations identify and analyze risks. These technologies can sift through massive volumes of data much faster than human analysts, identifying patterns and anomalies that may indicate potential vulnerabilities. For example, machine learning algorithms can analyze past incidents of data breaches, employee behaviour, and external threat indicators to build predictive models. These models can forecast the likelihood of various risks, allowing cybersecurity professionals to focus their efforts where they are needed most. With AI, organizations can automate the risk identification process, continuously learning from new data and adapting to emerging threats in real-time. This dynamic approach not only enhances the accuracy of risk assessments but also provides a more proactive stance in managing security challenges.

Despite its potential, the integration of machine learning and AI into risk management is not without challenges and ethical considerations. Organizations must grapple with data privacy issues, ensuring they comply with regulations while utilizing large amounts of sensitive information for training AI models. The reliance on automated systems can create a sense of complacency among cybersecurity professionals, who may overlook critical context that machines cannot fully comprehend. Furthermore, biases in the algorithms themselves can lead to flawed risk assessments. If an AI system is trained on biased data, it may disproportionately flag certain behaviours as risky while ignoring others, putting organizations at unforeseen risk. Establishing transparency in AI decision-making processes is crucial, as is fostering a culture where human expertise and machine intelligence work in tandem, rather than in isolation.

As organizations move towards automation in risk management, it is essential to remain vigilant about the balance between technology and human oversight. Continuous training of machine learning models is paramount to ensure they are equipped to handle the evolving nature of cyber threats. Regular audits and assessments of AI systems can help identify biases and inaccuracies, ensuring that the deployed technologies enhance rather than hinder risk management efforts. Cybersecurity professionals should also prioritize staying informed about advancements in AI, fostering a collaborative environment where technology complements human intuition, ultimately leading to more resilient security strategies.

14.2: The Impact of Quantum Computing

The future implications of quantum computing on cyber security risk management are profound. As quantum systems come of age, the landscape of risks will shift dramatically. Quantum computers possess the potential to solve complex problems much faster than classical computers. This includes breaking traditional encryption methods that secure sensitive data today. For cyber security professionals, this means reassessing current risk management strategies. Organizations must prepare for a paradigm shift where quantum attacks could compromise systems that were previously deemed secure. The timeline for this transition is uncertain, but experts predict that within the next decade, enterprises may need to adopt quantum-resistant encryption algorithms to safeguard their information assets effectively. Understanding the vulnerabilities and proactively updating or replacing existing cryptographic protocols will be essential in managing these emerging risks.

Advancements in quantum technology bring a double-edged sword of risks and opportunities. On one hand, there is the risk of quantum-enabled attacks that could de-anonymize data, compromise confidentiality, and disrupt entire infrastructures. Hackers could leverage quantum computing to bypass firewalls and security protocols that rely on the weakness of classical computation. On the other hand, quantum technology offers opportunities for enhanced security measures. Quantum key distribution (QKD), for example, uses the principles of quantum mechanics to create communication channels that are theoretically immune to eavesdropping. By using QKD, organizations can ensure that any attempt to intercept communications would be detectable. Balancing these risks and opportunities will require a continuous effort in education, adaptation, and the development of new security frameworks that incorporate quantum principles.

As discussions around quantum computing evolve, professionals in cyber security must remain vigilant and proactive. Engaging in interdisciplinary collaboration with quantum physicists, cryptographers, and IT specialists can provide valuable insights into developing risk management practices suited for the quantum era. Regular training sessions focused on the implications of quantum technology can also keep teams informed and prepared. Staying ahead in this rapidly advancing field is not just an option but a necessity for resilient cyber security management.

14.3: Evolving Cyber Security Landscape

Technological advancements and societal shifts have become the twin engines driving the evolution of the cyber threat landscape. As we have witnessed the rise of the Internet of Things (IoT), artificial intelligence, and cloud computing, the attack surface for malicious actors has expanded dramatically. More devices are connected than ever before, creating a vast playground for cyber criminals eager to exploit vulnerabilities. The proliferation of mobile technology has resulted in users demanding constant connectivity, which often sidelines security considerations. Coupled with the rise of social media, where personal information is easily shared and disseminated, attackers have more tools at their disposal to engineer sophisticated phishing schemes and social engineering attacks. Understanding these changes is crucial for cyber security professionals as they acknowledge that traditional security measures are often insufficient in the face of newly emerging threats.

Developing adaptive risk management strategies is essential in navigating this continuously shifting landscape. Cyber security professionals must prioritize a proactive rather than reactive approach to security. This involves implementing frameworks that are not only resilient but also flexible enough to adapt to new threats. Regularly updating security protocols and conducting threat assessments can ensure that vulnerabilities are addressed promptly. Collaboration among teams and departments can foster an environment where knowledge is shared and risks are collectively managed. Incorporating machine learning and analytics can provide insights into patterns of behaviour and potential threats, allowing organizations to stay a step ahead of potential attackers. Emphasizing an organizational culture that prioritizes security awareness will enhance the human element of risk management, as end-users are often the first line of defense against cyber threats.

Utilizing a risk-based approach, cyber security professionals should consider implementing a continuous monitoring strategy that incorporates real-time alerts to identify and respond to threats swiftly. By investing in automated security solutions, organizations can reduce the burden on their security teams while maintaining a high level of vigilance. Understanding compliance requirements is also critical, as regulatory frameworks are constantly evolving in response to the changing cyber landscape. Keeping abreast of these developments will not only mitigate risks but safeguard businesses' reputations and customer trust. Continuous learning and adaptation should be integral components of any successful cyber security strategy, enabling organizations to turn the tide against potential threats and establish a safer digital environment.

Chapter 15: Case Studies in Risk Management

15.1: Successful Risk Management Implementations

Successful implementations of risk management frameworks can be seen across various sectors, demonstrating the critical role that structured approaches play in mitigating threats. One notable case is a financial institution that adopted a comprehensive risk management framework to defend against increasing cyber threats. By integrating a risk assessment process into decision-making, the institution identified vulnerabilities in its data handling practices and implemented strict controls and staff training programs. This proactive stance not only fortified their defenses but also built a culture of awareness and responsibility among employees. Another compelling example comes from a healthcare organization that faced significant operational risks. The organization employed a real-time risk monitoring system, utilizing advanced analytics to assess and respond to potential incidents. By prioritizing risks based on their impact on patient care, they were able to direct resources effectively and ensure compliance with regulatory standards, ultimately enhancing patient trust and safety. These case studies exemplify the transformative impact of risk management frameworks when aligned with organizational goals.

From these success stories, several best practices emerge that cybersecurity professionals can adopt to optimize their own risk management strategies. Firstly, embedding a risk management culture within the organization is essential. This involves not only training employees but also encouraging open communication regarding risks and incidents. Secondly, leveraging technology effectively, such as employing AI and machine learning tools for risk assessment and data analysis, can provide real-time insights and facilitate faster decision-making. Collaboration across departments is also pivotal; cross-functional teams that combine expertise from IT, compliance, and business operations can better identify and manage risks that may not be apparent within silos. Additionally, regularly revisiting and updating the risk management framework ensures that it evolves in tandem with the organization's objectives and the external threat landscape. Engaging with external stakeholders, including customers and regulatory bodies, can also enhance transparency and trust, strengthening the organization's commitment to a robust risk management approach.

For cybersecurity professionals, one practical tip to enhance risk management implementation is to establish a KPI system that measures the effectiveness of risk-related activities. This could include metrics such as incident response times, the number of identified vulnerabilities, or employee participation in training programs. Monitoring these indicators allows organizations to gauge progress over time, identify areas for improvement, and demonstrate the value of their risk management initiatives to all stakeholders involved.

15.2: Lessons Learned from Cyber Incidents

Significant cyber incidents and breaches provide crucial lessons that can shape the future of information security. One key takeaway is the importance of a proactive rather than reactive stance. Many breaches, such as those experienced by major corporations, reveal that organizations often underestimate the sophistication of cyber threats. High-profile attacks like the Target data breach in 2013 highlighted vulnerabilities in third-party vendor management and the essential need for comprehensive risk assessments, which should include all points of entry into a system. The Equifax breach of 2017 serves as a stark reminder that timely patching of known vulnerabilities is critical. Delays can have catastrophic consequences, reminding us of the adage that the best defense is often an anticipatory one. Organizations must cultivate a culture of continuous improvement, learning from these incidents to refine processes, enhance training, and strengthen defenses.

These insights can significantly inform improvements in risk management strategies. By analyzing past breaches, cybersecurity professionals can better tailor their risk assessments to include emerging threats and vulnerabilities. For instance, the realization that many breaches stem from human error—such as phishing attacks—emphasizes the need for more rigorous training and awareness programs for employees. Risk management strategies can be enhanced by integrating threat intelligence into security protocols, ensuring that teams stay informed of current attack trends. Additionally, the consideration of scenario-based planning allows organizations to better prepare for and respond to potential incidents. By reflecting on the consequences of past breaches, professionals can develop more dynamic and adaptable risk management frameworks, enabling them to address both current and impending threats.

Staying vigilant in the face of evolving cyber threats should be a paramount objective for organizations. Practical steps, such as implementing regular drills and simulations based on recent incidents, can deepen understanding and readiness among staff. Establishing a feedback loop, where lessons learned are documented and shared organization-wide, ensures that knowledge is preserved and built upon. This proactive and informed approach helps create a resilient security posture capable of withstanding future challenges.

15.3: Industry-specific Risk Management Analyses

Risk management practices must be tailored to address the unique challenges of specific industries. Each sector operates under its distinct circumstances and regulatory environments, which necessitates specialized approaches to mitigate risks effectively. For example, in the healthcare sector, the primary focus often revolves around patient data protection and compliance with regulations such as HIPAA. Cybersecurity professionals must implement stringent access controls, encrypt sensitive medical records, and regularly conduct vulnerability assessments to safeguard patient confidentiality and maintain trust. In contrast, the financial services industry is heavily regulated and requires robust measures against fraud and data breaches, compelling cybersecurity experts to adopt solutions like advanced threat detection systems and continuous monitoring of transactions.

Comparative analyses reveal that while all industries face common risk management issues, their responses can dramatically differ based on operational priorities and the potential impact of risks. For instance, manufacturing might emphasize the physical security of machinery and operational continuity planning, whereas technology firms may prioritize securing intellectual property and protecting against advanced persistent threats. By dissecting these responses, cybersecurity professionals can learn from the strengths and weaknesses of various industries, identifying best practices that can be adapted across sectors. Networking with peers in different fields can provide invaluable insights into how risk is managed elsewhere, allowing for a more proactive approach to addressing threats and effectiveness in a given context.

Understanding how risk management varies by industry does not only help in crafting targeted strategies, but it also highlights the importance of continuous learning and adaptation. Cybersecurity professionals should engage in cross-industry forums and discussions to gather fresh perspectives on emerging threats and innovations in risk management techniques. This knowledge-sharing can lead to the development of a more resilient cybersecurity posture, regardless of the specific challenges faced within one's own industry. Adopting a well-rounded viewpoint around risk management can empower professionals to devise solutions that are not only effective but also innovative.